# Shakespeare Monologues for Women:

## Monologues for Getting into Drama School 2021

# CONTENTS

# INTRODUCTION

The monologue is a staple of all drama school applications. Whether you're applying for an acting course, or a mix of musical theatre, dance, music, or another specialty, it is highly likely you will be asked to perform a monologue.

This can seem an incredibly daunting task if you do not have a broad knowledge of a wide range of plays, especially when it comes to Ancient Greek theatre. To save you from reading hundreds of individual plays just to find a monologue that suits you, this book has done the work and gathered a collection of exciting pieces perfect for your drama school audition.

This edition of Monologues for Women: Getting into Drama School 2021 is packed full of pieces taken from Ancient Greece, featuring 60 monologues of varying length from 22 plays. There is something in this book for everyone. From Tragedy to Comedy. Find the monologue that is the right fit for you and break a leg!

# TIPS FOR PERFORMING MONOLOGUES

Performing monologues is a strange experience. Instead of being immersed in the set and costume of a full production in front of an audience, you are standing in a plain echoey audition room with a handful of audience members who are all there to judge you. You have to provide all the context and take your audience on an emotional journey within a very short space of time. It's an incredibly daunting task, but armed with a good monologue and these tips you should have the confidence to put on a great performance.

1. Read the play. This collection is an excellent starting point, but once you've found a monologue that resonates with you find a copy of the play it's from and read it cover to cover. Watch a performance of it if you can.
2. Study the context. Monologues don't come out of nowhere, even if it appears that way in the audition room. Know where you've come from, what just happened on stage, who you're talking to, and what your intentions are.
3. Prepare to take direction. So you've performed your monologue and you're very pleased with all the choices you've made, but now the audition panel is asking you to do something completely different. Be open to this! Directors aren't necessarily giving you the best choices for the piece, they're looking to see if you can follow instructions.

4. Enjoy yourself! A tense auditionee stands out and for all the wrong ways. Have confidence in yourself and have fun as you embody the character.

5. Stand still. It's distracting to watch a performer dart across the audition space or wave their hands around. Practice performing without moving at all, hands by your sides. You'll be surprised at the benefits it gives to your facial expressions and general emotion. A lot of us make habits and gestures while we're nervous, be comfortable performing in complete stillness.

6. Warm up properly. Warm up your voice with some simple exercises like humming, breathing, and scales. Massage your face and jaw and do some basic stretches. This will help relax you so you'll feel less tense.

7. Prepare for things to go wrong. Forgetting your lines happens to the best actors. Denzel Washington is famous for asking for lines whenever he performs onstage and he still gives incredible immersive performances. Unlike Denzel you won't have someone feeding you the script, but you can respond to forgetting lines in the same way. Stay in the moment, stay in character, keep going, don't let the pause get carried away. Making mistakes is natural, the directors will love to see how you deal with them.

8. Make eye contact, but also...don't make eye contact. This sounds confusing, but it does make sense. It can be uncomfortable to have someone performing a monologue directly at you, but at the same time it's strange to watch someone perform to the wall behind your head. Make eye contact with the audition panel as you enter, and when you perform your monologue pick a spot to look at, but occasionally make eye contact with the casting directors. It will keep you connected to them without being too intense, and you won't be performing blankly to a brick behind them.

9. Be original. Watch productions to get inspiration, but bear in mind the audition panel are likely familiar with the adaptations too. You want to stand out, be bold, and do something different. Make an

interesting unique choice that you haven't seen before. Let your personality shine through.

10. Don't pick something too obscure, and if you do make sure you have some popular supporting pieces. It's tempting to find a monologue the panel have never seen before, but remember that if they're hearing it for the first time they're taking in new information without focusing on you. A monologue that's familiar to the panel helps them focus just on your performance. All the monologues in this book have been chosen for their emotional power, some are more well known than others, make sure you do your research!

# All's Well that Ends Well

Helena

I confess

Here on my knee before high heaven and you,

That before you, and next unto high heaven,

I love your son.

My friends were poor but honest; so's my love.

Be not offended, for it hurts not him

That he is loved of me. I follow him not

By any token of presumptuous suit,

Nor would I have him till I do deserve him;

Yet never know how that desert should be.

I know I love in vain, strive against hope;

Yet in this captious and intensible sieve

I still pour in the waters of my love

And lack not to lose still. Thus, Indian-like,

Religious in mine error, I adore

The sun that looks upon his worshipper

But knows of him no more. My dearest madam,

Let not your hate encounter with my love,

For loving where you do; but if yourself,

Whose agèd honor cites a virtuous youth,

Did ever in so true a flame of liking,

Wish chastely and love dearly, that your Dian

Was both herself and Love, O, then give pity

To her whose state is such that cannot choose

But lend and give where she is sure to lose;

That seeks not to find that her search implies,

But, riddle-like, lives sweetly where she dies.

## As You Like It

Phebe

Think not I love him, though I ask for him;

'Tis but a peevish boy; yet he talks well.

But what care I for words? Yet words do well

When he that speaks them pleases those that hear.

It is a pretty youth; not very pretty;

But sure he's proud; and yet his pride becomes him.

He'll make a proper man. The best thing in him

Is his complexion; and faster than his tongue

Did make offense, his eye did heal it up.

He is not very tall; yet for his year's he's tall.

His leg is but so so; and yet 'tis well.

There was a pretty redness in his lip,

A little riper and more lusty red

Than that mixed in his cheek; 'twas just the difference

Betwixt the constant red and mingled damask.

There be some women, Silvius, had they marked him

In parcels as I did, would have gone near

To fall in love with him; but, for my part,

I love him not nor hate him not; and yet

I have more cause to hate him than to love him;

For what had he to do to chide at me?

He said mine eyes were black and my hair black;

And, now I am rememb'red, scorned at me.

I marvel why I answered not again.

But that's all one; omittance is no quittance.

I'll write to him a very taunting letter,

And thou shalt bear it. Wilt thou, Silvius?

# Henry VI Part II

Queen

Can you not see? or will ye not observe
The strangeness of his altered countenance?
With what a majesty he bears himself,
How insolent of late he is become,
How proud, how peremptory, and unlike himself?
We know the time since he was mild and affable,
And if we did but glance a far-off look,
Immediately he was upon his knee,
That all the court admired him for submission;
But meet him now and, be it in the morn,
When every one will give the time of day,
He knits his brow and shows an angry eye
And passeth by with stiff unbowèd knee,
Disdaining duty that to us belongs.
Small curs are not regarded when they grin,
But great men tremble when the lion roars,
And Humphrey is no little man in England.
First note that he is near you in descent,
And should you fall, he is the next will mount.

Me seemeth then it is no policy,

Respecting what a rancorous mind he bears

And his advantage following your decease,

That he should come about your royal person

Or be admitted to your highness' council.

By flattery hath he won the commons' heart;

And when he please to make commotion,

'Tis to be feared they all will follow him.

Now 'tis the spring, and weeds are shallow-rooted.

Suffer them now, and they'll o'ergrow the garden

And choke the herbs for want of husbandry.

The reverent care I bear unto my lord

Made me collect these dangers in the duke.

If it be fond, call it a woman's fear;

Which fear if better reasons can supplant,

I will subscribe and say I wronged the duke.

My Lord of Suffolk, Buckingham, and York,

Reprove my allegation if you can,

Or else conclude my words effectual.

Queen

Be woe for me, more wretched than he is.

What, dost thou turn away, and hide thy face?

I am no loathsome leper. Look on me.

What? Art thou like the adder waxen deaf?

Be poisonous too, and kill thy forlorn queen.

Is all thy comfort shut in Gloucester's tomb?

Why, then Dame Margaret was ne'er thy joy.

Erect his statue and worship it,

And make my image but an alehouse sign.

Was I for this nigh wracked upon the sea

And twice by awkward wind from England's bank

Drove back again unto my native clime?

What boded this but well-forewarning wind

Did seem to say, 'Seek not a scorpion's nest

Nor set no footing on this unkind shore'?

What did I then but cursed the gentle gusts

And he that loosed them forth their brazen caves,

And bid them blow toward England's blessèd shore

Or turn our stern upon a dreadful rock?

Yet Aeolus would not be a murderer,

But left that hateful office unto thee.

The pretty vaulting sea refused to drown me,

Knowing that thou wouldst have me drowned on shore

With tears as salt as sea through thy unkindness.

The splitting rocks cowered in the sinking sands

And would not dash me with their ragged sides,

Because they flinty heart, more hard than they,

Might in thy palace perish Margaret.

As far as I could ken thy chalky cliffs,

When from thy shore the tempest beat us back,

I stood upon the hatches in the storm,

And when the dusky sky began to rob

My earnest-gaping sight of thy land's view,

I took a costly jewel from my neck,

A heart it was, bound in with diamonds,

And threw it toward thy land. The sea received it,

And so I wished thy body might my heart;

And even with this I lost fair England's view,

And bid mine eyes be packing with my heart,

And called them blind and dusky spectacles

For losing ken of Albion's wishèd coast.

How often have I tempted Suffolk's tongue

(The agent of thy foul inconstancy)

To sit and witch me as Ascanius did

When he to madding Dido would unfold

His father's acts commenced in burning Troy!

Am I not witched like her? or thou not false like him?

Ay me, I can no more. Die, Margaret!

For Henry weeps that thou dost live so long.

# Macbeth

Hecate

Have I not reason, beldams as you are,

Saucy and overbold? How did you dare

To trade and traffic with Macbeth

In riddles and affairs of death;

And I, the mistress of your charms,

The close contriver of all harms,

Was never called to bear my part

Or show the glory of our art?

And, which is worse, all you have done

Hath been but for a wayward son,

Spiteful and wrathful, who, as others do,

Loves for his own ends, not for you.

But make amends now: get you gone

And at the pit of Acheron

Meet me i' th' morning. Thither he

Will come to know his destiny.

Your vessels and your spells provide,

Your charms and everything beside.

I am for th' air. This night I'll spend

Unto a dismal and a fatal end.

Great business must be wrought ere noon.

Upon the corner of the moon

There hangs a vap'rous drop profound;

I'll catch it ere it come to ground:

And that, distilled by magic sleights,

Shall raise such artificial sprites

As by the strength of their illusion

Shall draw him on to his confusion.

He shall spurn fate, scorn death, and bear

His hopes 'bove wisdom, grace, and fear:

And you all know security

Is mortals' chiefest enemy.


[Music, and a song.]


Hark! I am called. My little spirit, see,

Sits in a foggy cloud and stays for me.

Lady Macbeth


He has almost supped.

Why have you left the chamber?

Was the hope drunk

Wherein you dressed yourself? Hath it slept since?

And wakes it now to look so green and pale

At what it did so freely? From this time

Such I account thy love. Art thou afeard

To be the same in thine own act and valor

As thou art in desire? Wouldst thou have that

Which thou esteem'st the ornament of life,

And live a coward in thine own esteem,

Letting "I dare not" wait upon "I would,"

Like the poor cat i' the adage?

What beast was't then

That made you break this enterprise to me?

When you durst do it, then you were a man;

And to be more than what you were, you would

Be so much more the man. Nor time nor place

Did then adhere, and yet you would make both.

They have made themselves, and that their fitness now

Does unmake you. I have given suck, and know

How tender 'tis to love the babe that milks me:

I would, while it was smiling in my face,

Have plucked my nipple from his boneless gums

And dashed the brains out, had I so sworn as you

Have done this. If we should fail?

Screw your courage to the sticking place

And we'll not fail. When Duncan is asleep

(Whereto the rather shall his day's hard journey

Soundly invite him), his two chamberlains

Will I with wine and wassail so convince

That memory, the warder of the brain,

Shall be a fume, and the receipt of reason

A limbeck only. When in swinish sleep

Their drenchèd natures lies as in a death,

What cannot you and I perform upon

Th' unguarded Duncan? what not put upon

His spongy officers, who shall bear the guilt

Of our great quell?

# A Midsummer Night's Dream

Helena

How happy some o'er other some can be!

Through Athens I am thought as fair as she.

But what of that? Demetrius thinks not so;

He will not know what all but he do know.

And as he errs, doting on Hermia's eyes,

So I, admiring of his qualities.

Things base and vile, holding no quantity,

Love can transpose to form and dignity.

Love looks not with the eyes, but with the mind,

And therefore is winged Cupid painted blind.

Nor hath Love's mind of any judgment taste;

Wings, and no eyes, figure unheedy haste.

And therefore is Love said to be a child,

Because in choice he is so oft beguiled.

As waggish boys in game themselves forswear,

So the boy Love is perjured everywhere.

For ere Demetrius looked on Hermia's eyne,

He hailed down oaths that he was only mine;

And when this hail some heat from Hermia felt,

So he dissolved, and show'rs of oaths did melt.

I will go tell him of fair Hermia's flight.

Then to the wood will he to-morrow night

Pursue her; and for this intelligence

If I have thanks, it is a dear expense.

But herein mean I to enrich my pain,

To have his sight thither and back again.

# The Comedy of Errors

Adriana

Ay, ay, Antipholus, look strange and frown.

Some other mistress hath thy sweet aspects;

I am not Adriana, nor thy wife.

The time was once when thou unurged wouldst vow

That never words were music to thine ear,

That never object pleasing in thine eye,

That never touch well welcome to thy hand,

That never meat sweet-savored in thy taste,

Unless I spake, or looked, or touched, or carved to thee.

How comes it now, my husband, O, how comes it,

That thou art then estrangèd from thyself?

Thyself I call it, being strange to me,

That, undividable, incorporate,

Am better than thy dear self's better part.

Ah, do not tear away thyself from me!

For know, my love, as easy mayst thou fall

A drop of water in the breaking gulf,

And take unmingled thence that drop again

Without addition of diminishing,

As take from me thyself and not me too.

How dearly would it touch thee to the quick,

Shouldst thou but hear I were licentious,

And that this body, consecrate to thee,

By ruffian lust should be contaminate!

Wouldst thou not spit at me, and spurn at me,

And hurl the name of husband in my face,

And tear the stained skin off my harlot-brow,

And from my false hand cut the wedding-ring,

And break it with a deep-divorcing vow?

I know thou canst, and therefore see thou do it.

I am possessed with an adulterate blot;

My blood is mingled with the crime of lust.

For if we two be one, and thou play false,

I do digest the poison of thy flesh,

Being strumpeted by thy contagion.

Keep then fair league and truce with thy true bed;

I live disdained, thou undishonorèd.

# Coriolanus

Volumnia

You are too absolute;

Though therein you can never be too noble,

But when extremities speak. I have heard you say,

Honor and policy, like unsevered friends,

I' th' war do grow together. Grant that, and tell me,

In peace what each of them by th' other lose,

That they combine not there.

If it be honor in your wars to seem

The same you are not, -- which, for your best ends,

You adopt your policy -- how is it less or worse,

That it shall hold companionship in peace

With honor, as in war; since that to both

It stands in like request?

It lies on you to speak

To th' people, not by your own instruction,

Nor by th' matter which your heart prompts you,

But with such words that are but roted in

Your tongue, though but bastards and syllables

Of no allowance to your bosom's truth.

Now, this no more dishonors you at all

Than to take in a town with gentle words,

Which else would put you to your fortune and

The hazard of much blood.

I would dissemble with my nature where

My fortunes and my friends at stake required

I should do so in honor. I am in this

Your wife, your son, these senators, the nobles;

And you will rather show our general louts

How you can frown than spend a fawn upon 'em,

For the inheritance of their loves and safeguard

Of what that want might ruin.

I prithee now, my son,

Go to them, with this bonnet in thy hand;

And thus far having stretched it, -- here be with them --

Thy knee bussing the stones, -- for in such business

Action is eloquence, and the eyes of th' ignorant

More learned than the ears -- waving thy head,

Which, often thus correcting thy stout heart,

Now humble as the ripest mulberry

That will not hold the handling; or say to them

Thou art their soldier, and being bred in broils

Hast not the soft way which, thou dost confess,

Were fit for thee to use as they to claim,

In asking their good loves; but thou wilt frame

Thyself, forsooth, hereafter theirs, so far

As thou hast power and person.

Go and be ruled; although I know thou hadst rather

Follow thine enemy in a fiery gulf

Than flatter him in a bower.

Volumnia

O, no more, no more!
You have said you will not grant us anything;
For we have nothing else to ask but that
Which you deny already; yet we will ask,
That, if you fail in our request, the blame
May hang upon your hardness. Think with thyself
How more unfortunate than all living women
Are we come hither; since that thy sight, which should
Make our eyes flow with joy, hearts dance with comforts,
Constrains them weep and shake with fear and sorrow,
Making the mother, wife, and child to see
The son, the husband, and the father tearing
His country's bowels out. And to poor we
Thine enmity's most capital. Thou barr'st us
Our prayers to the gods, which is a comfort
That all but we enjoy. For how can we,
Alas, how can we for our country pray,
Whereto we are bound, together with thy victory,
Whereto we are bound? Alack, or we must lose
The country, our dear nurse, or else thy person,
Our comfort in the country. We must find

An evident calamity, though we had

Our wish which side should win. For either thou

Must as a foreign recreant be led

With manacles through our streets, or else

Triumphantly tread on thy country's ruin,

And bear the palm for having bravely shed

Thy wife and children's blood. For myself, son,

I purpose not to wait on fortune till

These wars determine. If I cannot persuade thee

Rather to show a noble grace to both parts

Than seek the end of one, thou shalt no sooner

March to assault thy country than to tread--

Trust to 't, thou shalt not -- on thy mother's womb

That brought thee to this world.

# Richard III

Queen Margaret

If ancient sorrow be most reverent,
Give mine the benefit of seniory
And let my griefs frown on the upper hand.
If sorrow can admit society,
Tell over your woes again by viewing mine.
I had an Edward, till a Richard killed him;
I had a Harry, till a Richard killed him:
Thou hadst an Edward, till a Richard killed him;
Thou hadst a Richard, till a Richard killed him.
Thou hadst a Clarence too, and Richard killed him.
From forth the kennel of thy womb hath crept
A hellhound that doth hunt us all to death:
That dog, that had his teeth before his eyes,
To worry lambs and lap their gentle blood,
That foul defacer of God's handiwork,
That excellent grand tyrant of the earth
That reigns in gallèd eyes of weeping souls,
Thy womb let loose to chase us to our graves.
O upright, just, and true-disposing God,

29

How do I thank thee that this carnal cur

Preys on the issue of his mother's body

And makes her pew-fellow with others' moan!

Bear with me! I am hungry for revenge,

And now I cloy me with beholding it.

Thy Edward he is dead, that killed my Edward;

Thy other Edward dead, to quit my Edward;

Young York he is but boot, because both they

Matched not the high perfection of my loss.

Thy Clarence he is dead that stabbed my Edward,

And the beholders of this frantic play,

Th' adulterate Hastings, Rivers, Vaughan, Grey,

Untimely smoth'red in their dusky graves.

Richard yet lives, hell's black intelligencer;

Only reserved their factor to buy souls

And send them thither. But at hand, at hand,

Ensues his piteous and unpitied end.

Earth gapes, hell burns, fiends roar, saints pray,

To have him suddenly conveyed from hence.

Cancel his bond of life, dear God, I pray,

That I may live and say, 'The dog is dead.'

I called thee once vain flourish of my fortune;

I called thee then poor shadow, painted queen,

The presentation of but what I was,

The flattering index of a direful pageant,

One heaved a-high to be hurled down below,

A mother only mocked with two fair babes,

A dream of what thou wast, a garish flag,

To be the aim of every dangerous shot;

A sign of dignity, a breath, a bubble,

A queen in jest, only to fill the scene.

Where is thy husband now? Where be thy brothers?

Where be thy two sons? Wherein dost thou joy?

Who sues and kneels and says, 'God save the queen'?

Where be the bending peers that flatterèd thee?

Where be the thronging troops that followèd thee?

Decline all this, and see what now thou art:

For happy wife, a most distressèd widow;

For joyful mother, one that wails the name;

For one being sued to, one that humbly sues;

For queen, a very caitiff crowned with care;

For she that scorned at me, now scorned of me;

For she being feared of all, now fearing one;

For she commanding all, obeyed of none.

Thus hath the course of justice whirled about

And left thee but a very prey to time,

Having no more but thought of what thou wast,

To torture thee the more, being what thou art.

31

Thou didst usurp my place, and dost thou not

Usurp the just proportion of my sorrow?

Now thy proud neck bears half my burdened yoke,

From which even here I slip my weary head

And leave the burden of it all on thee.

Farewell, York's wife, and queen of sad mischance!

These English woes shall make me smile in France.

## Romeo and Juliet

Nurse

Even or odd, of all days in the year,

Come Lammas Eve at night shall she be fourteen.

Susan and she (God rest all Christian souls!)

Were of an age. Well, Susan is with God;

She was too good for me. But, as I said,

On Lammas Eve at night shall she be fourteen;

That shall she, marry; I remember it well.

'Tis since the earthquake now eleven years;

And she was weaned (I never shall forget it),

Of all the days of the year, upon that day;

For I had then laid wormwood to my dug,

Sitting in the sun under the dovehouse wall.

My lord and you were then at Mantua.

Nay, I do bear a brain. But, as I said,

When it did taste the wormwood on the nipple

Of my dug and felt it bitter, pretty fool,

To see it tetchy and fall out with the dug!

Shake, quoth the dovehouse! 'Twas no need, I trow,

To bid me trudge.

And since that time it is eleven years,

For then she could stand high-lone; nay, by th' rood,

She could have run and waddled all about;

For even the day before, she broke her brow;

And then my husband (God be with his soul!

'A was a merry man) took up the child.

'Yea,' quoth he, 'dost thou fall upon thy face?

Thou wilt fall backward when thou hast more wit;

Wilt thou not, Jule?' and, by my holidam,

The pretty wretch left crying and said 'Ay.'

To see now how a jest shall come about!

I warrant, an I should live a thousand years

I never should forget it. 'Wilt thou not, Jule?' quoth he,

And, pretty fool, it stinted and said 'Ay.'

Juliet

Thou knowest the mask of night is on my face;

Else would a maiden blush bepaint my cheek

For that which thou hast heard me speak to-night.

Fain would I dwell on form -- fain, fain deny

What I have spoke; but farewell compliment!

Dost thou love me? I know thou wilt say 'Ay';

And I will take thy word. Yet, if thou swear'st,

Thou mayst prove false. At lovers' perjuries,

They say Jove laughs. O gentle Romeo,

If thou dost love, pronounce it faithfully.

Or if thou thinkest I am too quickly won,

I'll frown, and be perverse, and say thee nay,

So thou wilt woo; but else, not for the world.

In truth, fair Montague, I am too fond,

And therefore thou mayst think my havior light;

But trust me, gentleman, I'll prove more true

Than those that have more cunning to be strange.

I should have been more strange, I must confess,

But that thou overheard'st, ere I was ware,

My true-love passion. Therefore pardon me,

And not impute this yielding to light love,

Which the dark night hath so discovered.

## Titus Andronicus

Tamora

Have I not reason, think you, to look pale?
These two have ticed me hither to this place,
A barren detested vale you see it is;
The trees, though summer, yet forlorn and lean,
Overcome with moss and baleful mistletoe.
Here never shines the sun; here nothing breeds,
Unless the nightly owl or fatal raven:
And when they showed me this abhorrèd pit,
They told me, here, at dead time of the night,
A thousand fiends, a thousand hissing snakes,
Ten thousand swelling toads, as many urchins,
Would make such fearful and confusèd cries
As any mortal body hearing it
Should straight fall mad, or else die suddenly.
No sooner had they told this hellish tale
But straight they told me they would bind me here
Unto the body of a dismal yew
And leave me to this miserable death.
And then they called me foul adulteress,

Lascivious Goth, and all the bitterest terms

That ever ear did hear to such effect;

And had you not by wondrous fortune come,

This vengeance on me had they executed.

Revenge it, as you love your mother's life,

Or be ye not henceforth called my children.

# Henry IV Part I

Lady Percy

O my good lord, why are you thus alone?
For what offense have I this fortnight been
A banished woman from my Harry's bed?
Tell me, sweet lord, what is't that takes from thee
Thy stomach, pleasure, and thy golden sleep?
Why dost thou bend thine eyes upon the earth,
And start so often when thou sit'st alone?
Why hast thou lost the fresh blood in thy cheeks
And given my treasures and my rights of thee
To thick-eyed musing and cursed melancholy?
In thy faint slumbers I by thee have watched,
And heard thee murmur tales of iron wars,
Speak terms of manage to thy bounding steed,
Cry 'Courage! to the field!' And thou hast talked
Of sallies and retires, of trenches, tents,
Of palisadoes, frontiers, parapets,
Of basilisks, of cannon, culverin,
Of prisoners' ransom, and of soldiers slain,
And all the currents of a heady fight.

Thy spirit within thee hath been so at war,

And thus hath so bestirred thee in thy sleep,

That beads of sweat have stood upon thy brow

Like bubbles in a late-disturbèd stream,

And in thy face strange motions have appeared,

Such as we see when men restrain their breath

On some great sudden hest. O, what portents are these?

Some heavy business hath my lord in hand,

And I must know it, else he loves me not.

## Henry VIII

Katherine

Sir, I desire you do me right and justice,

And to bestow your pity on me; for

I am a most poor woman and a stranger,

Born out of your dominions: having here

No judge indifferent, nor no more assurance

Of equal friendship and proceeding. Alas, sir,

In what have I offended you? What cause

Hath my behavior given to your displeasure

That thus you should proceed to put me off

And take your good grace from me? Heaven witness,

I have been to you a true and humble wife,

At all times to your will conformable,

Even in fear to kindle your dislike,

Yea, subject to your countenance--glad or sorry

As I saw it inclined. When was the hour

I ever contradicted your desire

Or made it not mine too? Or which of your friends

Have I not strove to love, although I knew

He were mine enemy? What friend of mine

That had to him derived your anger, did I

Continue in my liking? nay, gave notice

He was from thence discharged? Sir, call to mind

That I have been your wife in this obedience

Upward of twenty years, and have been blest

With many children by you. If in the course

And process of this time you can report,

And prove it too, against mine honor aught,

My bond to wedlock, or my love and duty

Against your sacred person, in God's name

Turn me away, and let the foul'st contempt

Shut door upon me, and so give me up

To the sharp'st kind of justice. Please you, sir,

The king your father was reputed for

A prince most prudent, of an excellent

And unmatched wit and judgment. Ferdinand,

My father, King of Spain, was reckoned one

The wisest prince that there had reigned by many

A year before. It is not to be questioned

That they had gathered a wise council to them

Of every realm, that did debate this business,

Who deemed our marriage lawful. Wherefore I humbly

Beseech you, sir, to spare me till I may

Be by my friends in Spain advised, whose counsel

I will implore. If not, i' th' name of God,
Your pleasure be fulfilled!

# Twelfth Night

Viola

I left no ring with her. What means this lady?

Fortune forbid my outside have not charmed her.

She made good view of me; indeed, so much

That, as methought, her eyes had lost her tongue,

For she did speak in starts distractedly.

She loves me sure; the cunning of her passion

Invites me in this churlish messenger.

None of my lord's ring? Why, he sent her none.

I am the man. If it be so, as 'tis,

Poor lady, she were better love a dream.

Disguise, I see thou art a wickedness

Wherein the pregnant enemy does much.

How easy is it for the proper false

In women's waxen hearts to set their forms!

Alas, our frailty is the cause, not we,

For such as we are made of, such we be.

How will this fadge? My master loves her dearly;

And I (poor monster) fond as much on him;

And she (mistaken) seems to dote on me.

What will become of this? As I am man,

My state is desperate for my master's love.

As I am woman (now alas the day!),

What thriftless sighs shall poor Olivia breathe?

O Time, thou must untangle this, not I;

It is too hard a knot for me t' untie.

## The Winter's Tale

Hermione

Since what I am to say must be but that

Which contradicts my accusation, and

The testimony on my part no other

But what comes from myself, it shall scarce boot me

To say, "Not guilty." Mine integrity,

Being counted falsehood, shall, as I express it,

Be so received. But thus: if powers divine

Behold our human actions, as they do,

I doubt not then but innocence shall make

False accusation blush and tyranny

Tremble at patience. You, my lord, best know,

Who least will seem to do so, my past life

Hath been as continent, as chaste, as true,

As I am now unhappy; which is more

Than history can pattern, though devised

And played to take spectators. For behold me--

A fellow of the royal bed, which owe

A moiety of the throne, a great king's daughter,

The mother to a hopeful prince -- here standing

To prate and talk for life and honor 'fore

Who please to come and hear. For life, I prize it

As I weigh grief, which I would spare. For honor,

'Tis a derivative from me to mine,

And only that I stand for. I appeal

To your own conscience, sir, before Polixenes

Came to your court, how I was in your grace,

How merited to be so; since he came,

With what encounter so uncurrent I

Have strained t' appear thus; if one jot beyond

The bound of honor, or in act or will

That way inclining, hardened be the hearts

Of all that hear me, and my near'st of kin

Cry fie upon my grave!

Printed in Great Britain
by Amazon

69289351R00031